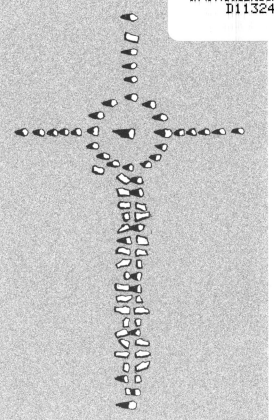

First published 2002 AD
© Wooden Books Ltd 2002 AD

Published by Wooden Books Ltd.
Walkmill, Cascob, Presteigne, Powys, Wales LD8 2NT

British Library Cataloguing in Publication Data
Ponting, G.
Callanish

A CIP catalogue record for this book is
available from the British Library

ISBN 1 904263 08 9

Printed and bound in Great Britain
by The Cromwell Press, Trowbridge

CALLANISH

AND OTHER MEGALITHIC SITES
OF THE OUTER HEBRIDES

by

Gerald Ponting

Dedicated to the memory of my colleague, friend and
mentor during my years on the Isle of Lewis, Dr. Alastair Fraser.

I originally researched the antiquarian and astronomical material on Callanish in 1975-84, when living a mile from the site. My partner in these investigations was then my wife, now Mrs Margaret Curtis. As co-authors, we recorded our findings in guide books to the sites, in several technical papers and in two unpublished volumes (see page 58). My thanks go to all who helped at that time, including Western Isles Libraries, local residents and the many archaeologists and other 'stones enthusiasts' who visited us in Lewis.

For material in this book and permission to reproduce it, thanks are due to: National Monuments Record of Scotland, Edinburgh (27 upper); National Library of Scotland, Edinburgh (this page, 11, 21 upper, 39, 47, 49 upper); Nationalmuseet, Copenhagen (16,17); University of St Andrews Library (33); Public Record Office, Kew (29 lower, 49 lower); Ordnance Survey, Southampton (23); Wiltshire Archaeological Society, Devizes (13); Oliver and Boyd (title page, 31 lower); Edinburgh University Press (6, 7 lower); Patrick Ashmore of Historic Scotland (9); and Gail Kelly (35 lower). The back cover illustration is taken from a paper by T.A.Wise (1877).

The Chandler's Ford branch of the Hampshire Library Service has kindly obtained many obscure books through the Inter-Library Service. I would like to thank my wife Elizabeth and also John Martineau and Katie L'Estrange of Wooden Books for all the effort put into the original drawings in this book.

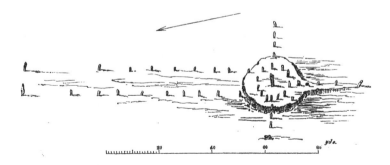

Callanish

← Ring of Brodgar

o Loanhead
of Daviot

o Castlerigg

Arbor
o Low

Rollright
o

Avebury
o

o Stonehenge

Stanton Drew

INTRODUCTION

Stonehenge is justifiably world-famous, but far to the north in the Outer Hebrides stands a monument just as worthy of attention. Indeed, the Standing Stones of Callanish are sometimes called the 'Stonehenge of the Hebrides'. For visitors who travel to appreciate its grandeur, its remoteness adds to its romance.

Callanish and Stonehenge are incredible survivors from a 'megalithic culture' which stretched the length of the British Isles. Brodgar in Orkney, Castlerigg in the Lake District and Rollright in Oxfordshire date from the same prehistoric era, as do around a thousand others. Many are now ruinous and an unknown number have been lost or destroyed.

Approaching Callanish across the moorlands from Stornoway, the stones appear silhouetted along a ridge. Standing among the stones, the visitor becomes aware of the vast open hemisphere of the sky. There seems little doubt that the sun and especially the moon had parts to play in whatever ancient dramas were enacted here.

Callanish is unique among settings of standing stones, having often been compared to the shape of a Celtic cross. Thirteen stones, between 8 and 12 feet tall, form a ring with a maximum diameter of only 41 feet, being slightly flattened on the east side. An impressive megalith, almost 16 feet tall, stands at the centre, set at one end of a burial chamber.

Three rows lead away from the circle, approximately to the east and west, and more precisely to the south. Three stones are additional to this pattern (*9, 34 and 35, opposite*). There is also a longer northerly avenue. The monument measures 400 feet north to south and 150 feet east to west. To the south is the natural rocky outcrop of Cnoc an Tursa.

The standing stones are composed of Lewisian gneiss and may have been transported no more than a mile. The builders probably chose shapes for aesthetic or magical reasons; stones with crystalline nodules were especially favoured.

As this book reveals, many writers have recorded their opinions about Callanish. However, the motives of those who laboured to create it, perhaps 5000 years ago, may never be known. Its continuing mystery is part of the attraction of the 'Stonehenge of the Hebrides'.

Chandler's Ford, 2002

Note: Historic Scotland has adopted the spelling *Calanais*, a Gaelicised version of a name that was never originally Gaelic. The word probably derives from *Kallaðarnes*, which signifies 'the promontory from which a ferry is called' in Old Norse, the language of the Vikings. Great Bernera was formerly reached by ferry from Callanish.

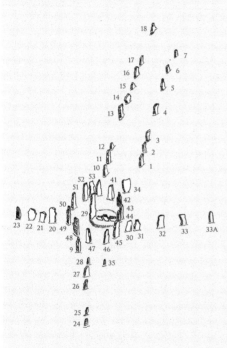

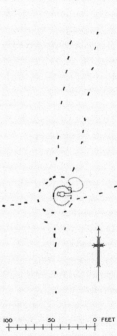

Plan above adapted from *RCAHMS Inventory, 1928*.
Stone numbers from Somerville, 1912.
Slabs of Cairn (not shown), nos. 36-40.

J. G. Callander's plan, published in
the RCAHMS Inventory of 1928

THE PREHISTORIC ENVIRONMENT
warm and dry in the Neolithic

The Isle of Lewis seems a remote and unlikely place for prehistoric peoples to have settled and built one of their greatest monuments. The modern visitor finds stretches of rolling, treeless moorland, inhabited only by hardy black-faced sheep. The coastline varies between spectacular rocky shores and sweeping pristine beaches of white sand.

Inland from these beaches, the sandy machair has relatively fertile soil. Most known prehistoric settlement sites, including that at Dalmore, nine miles to the north, were on the machair.

Lewis today suffers frequent winter gales and high rainfall. But in the Neolithic, or New Stone Age, the island was warmer, drier and less windy. Sea level was lower, so the sea-loch to the south of Callanish would have been mainly dry land.

Studies of pollen, preserved deep in the peat, show that hazel and silver birch grew near Callanish. Around 1550 BC, trees were cleared and cereal cultivation began – but undoubtedly there were settlements earlier than this known date.

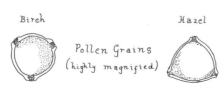

Birch   Hazel

Pollen Grains
(highly magnified)

THE OUTER HEBRIDES

Butt of Lewis

LEWIS

Stornoway
CALLANISH

N. HARRIS

Tarbert
S HARRIS

N. UIST
Lochmaddy

Balivanich
BENBECULA

S. UIST

Lochboisdale

BARRA

Castle bay

Barra
Head

20 miles

THE POWER OF A CHIEF
the social context of Callanish

At Callanish, as at other stone circles, information is sparse about its social context. Undoubtedly the people supported themselves by keeping livestock and growing grain which they ground for flour. They hunted, and used the harvest of the sea.

Their pottery vessels were richly decorated (*similar to those opposite*). They made tools of bone and stone, obtaining stone for their axes via far-flung trade routes. An axe, found in the peat in Lewis in 1983, was composed of porcellanite from Ireland. Its wooden handle was remarkably well preserved (*below*).

There is no certain trace of their houses, probably because the materials, such as turf and wood, leave little evidence today. In contrast, their stone monuments have stood through five millennia of Hebridean weather.

The creation of impressive monuments like Callanish would have emphasised the power of chieftains or priests and increased the cohesion of the local society. However, the many similarities in design between stone circles throughout Britain suggest frequent communication between widely scattered communities.

Phases of Construction
five thousand years at Callanish

A major excavation took place at Callanish in 1980 and 1981, directed by Patrick Ashmore, who distinguished several phases of activity (*see his impressions opposite*).

– In around 3000 BC early farmers ploughed the soil, which later developed into pasture.

– Holes were dug, probably to erect wooden posts to form a 'ritual enclosure' – or perhaps just a pen for stock.

– Fourteen megaliths were erected as a circle with a central stone (*upper drawing*). Small stones and clay were built into a mound around each stone to compensate for the shallowness of the socket holes. Probably the rows were added later, but there is no evidence to prove this.

– Centuries later, the chambers of the cairn were constructed on a specially levelled area. A circular kerb was added a little later (*lower drawing*).

– Around 1000 BC the capstones were thrown off the cairn and its contents scattered. Land within and around the circle was ploughed. Another culture with different beliefs may have taken over.

– Strangely, the cairn was then partially rebuilt, using former capstones to make a northern kerb. Not long after this, peat began to form, burying the cairn over the next 3000 years.

INCHANTERS AND DRUIDS
the earliest writers on Callanish

In *A Description of the Lewis by John Morisone Indweller There*, published around 1680, Callanish was first mentioned in print, though not named:

> "... there are great stones standing up in ranks, some two or three foot thick and 10, 12 and 15 foot high; It is left by traditione that these were a sort of men converted into stones by ane Inchanter ...

Some twenty years later, Martin Martin produced the first plan of the site (*opposite*). It was extremely inaccurate, with far too many stones in the avenue and only three in each of the other rows. His plan did not even match his written description, which gave four stones each in the S, E and W rows.

Martin reported that local people claimed that Callanish was

> "... a Place appointed for Worship in the time of Heathenism, and that the Chief Druid or Priest stood near the big Stone in the center, from whence he address'd himself to the People ..."

Later writers repeated Martin's ideas about Druids – and uncritically redrew his plan. The plan in James Logan's *The Scottish Gael* (1831), while improved in other respects, still included 19 stones on each side of the avenue (*see frontispiece*). Years after more accurate material had been published, the plan was unchanged in Logan's second edition of 1863.

The Form of ÿ Heathen Temple

THE FAMOUS ANTIQUARIAN
Callanish as a 'serpentine temple'

William Stukeley's careful drawings of the great stone circles of Wiltshire, made in the 1720s, are greatly valued today (see *Avebury* in this series). Stukeley's later publications are full of fanciful Druid theories, which nevertheless were very influential for many years. At Avebury, he considered the circle and curved avenues to represent a Druidical 'dracontium' or serpentine temple.

The manuscript plan of Callanish in his *Commonplace Book* was not original, Stukeley never having visited Scotland. He wrote:

> 'I took a drawing of it from Mr Llwdd's travels but he is a very bad designer … A part of the snake remains going from it which he calls an avenue. He did not discern the curve of it …'.

Edward Llwdd (or Lhwyd), whose work is lost, had copied Martin – and it is hardly surprising that he did not notice the curve of the straight Callanish avenue! Stukeley was trying to adjust the facts to fit his theories.

The similarity of the ground plan of Callanish to the shape of a Celtic Cross was noted by Rev. Thomas MacLaughlan in 1863. He speculated that the site was a 'Christian relic', perhaps built as a penance for a grievous sin!

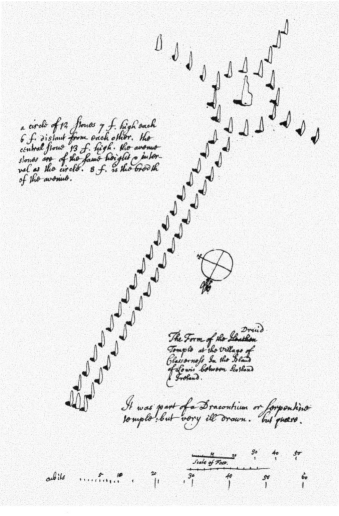

a circle of 12 stones 7 f. high each 6 f. distant from each other. the central stone 13 f. high. the avenue stones are of the same height & interval as the circle. 8 f. is the breadth of the avenue.

The Form of the Druid Temple at the village of Classerness In the Island of Lewis between Scotland & Ireland.

It was part of a Dracontium or serpentine temple: but very ill drawn. but quære.

Scale of Feet.
                    10   20   30   40   50

cubits 5 10   20   30   40   50   60

13

A BLANKET OF PEAT
is Callanish a 'restored site'?

By the Iron Age, the climate had deteriorated, and conditions on Lewis were cooler and damper. This resulted in the accumulation of layers of peat, which consists of partially decomposed plant material. By the nineteenth century, much of the island was blanketed in peat to a depth of five or six feet.

At Callanish, the stones thus looked much shorter than they do today. This was reflected in John MacCulloch's plan of 1819 (*opposite*), which shows a number of 'fallen stones'. At least eight of these are standing today, causing later writers to assume their re-erection and to call Callanish a 'restored site'.

MacCulloch's plan has to be interpreted along with drawings made by Tomkin in 1855, after the peat was cleared – but while bleaching of the stones still showed its former depth. Stone 3 had only its top edge exposed in 1819 (*below*) and MacCulloch must have thought he was looking at a much smaller stone, lying on its side. Far from being a restored site, it is now obvious that Callanish was protected, over two or three millennia, by enveloping peat.

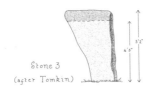

Stone 3
(after Tomkin)

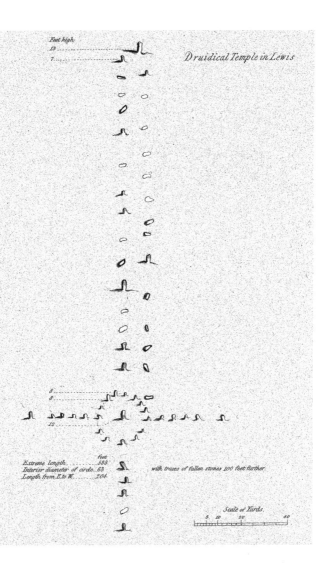

Feet high

13

7

Druidical Temple in Lewis

6

8

12

Extreme length 588
Interior diameter of circle .. 63
Length from E. to W. 204

feet

with traces of fallen stones 100 feet further.

Scale of Yards.
5   10   20   40

ANTIQUARIANS & ARCHÆOLOGISTS
a helpful Danish visitor

One of the limitations of the early antiquarians was the lack of a chronological framework for the past. Then, in 1851, Daniel Wilson published *Prehistoric Annals of Scotland*. (The second edition included an engraving of Callanish - *see page 35*). This was the first use of the word 'prehistoric' in English. A Danish professor, Christian Thomsen, had first divided ancient times into Ages of, successively, Stone, Bronze and Iron. So it is perhaps appropriate that the earliest known illustrations of Callanish were drawn by an early archaeologist from Denmark.

A sketch by Jacob Worsaae (*opposite above*), in an 1846 field notebook, confirms the conclusion from the MacCulloch and Tomkin material. Worsaae clearly showed the stones of the circle looking short; he was standing on a ground level five feet higher than today's, due to the blanketing peat.

A second sketch (*opposite below*), looking south towards the circle, shows that the ground level had already been lowered along most of the length of the avenue by peat cutting.

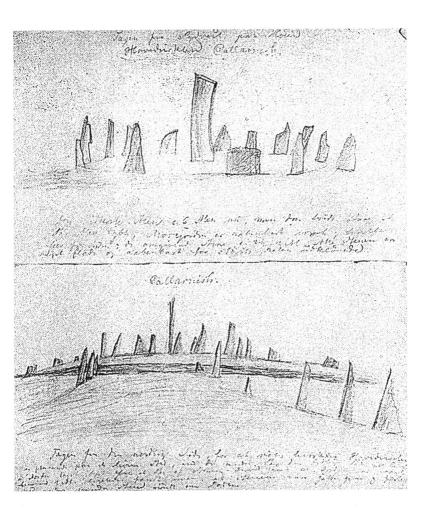

Tegen fra Søydenit (paa Hebel)
Hvredirkland Callernos?

Den ... Steen c.6. Alen ... ... den ... ...
... ... Morgoniden in ... ...
... ... Stenen en
... ...

Callarnish.

Tegen fra den nordre Side, for at vise, hvorledes Stenene ...
... ...
... ...
... ...

17

The 'Excavation' of 1857
rapid removal of five feet of peat

Henry Callender's paper of 1854 *Notice of the Stone Circle at Callernish* included the 'bird's eye view' (*opposite the contents page*) and a superb engraving by James Kerr (*below*). Villagers are seen gathering fuel by cutting peats across the east row; they could be expected to cut around the circle stones within a few

years. Therefore Callender suggested that the Society of Antiquaries should apply to Sir James Matheson, the owner of the Isle of Lewis, for "... the moss to be removed, so as ... to ascertain ... whether any building had been erected at the original level".

The peat was cleared on October 2nd 1857. Cosmo Innes reported to the Society that, five feet down, the workmen came upon "... a chambered building of three compartments".

THE BURIAL CHAMBER
exciting discovery beneath the peat

The 'chambered building' exactly fitted the small space between the central stone and the eastern–most stones of the circle, as shown in the plan from Innes' paper (*opposite, top*). It was clearly a small burial cairn, surrounded by a circular kerb and containing two roofless compartments and a short passage.

In describing the 1857 'excavation', Sir James Matheson stated: "It is remarkable that the sides of the small chamber are quite undisturbed". (Careful examination in 1981 showed that, in fact, some reconstruction must have taken place, as Victorian glass was found between the stones forming the sides of the chamber.)

With his note, Sir James enclosed "... some minute fragments of what we suppose to be bones found in the chamber, and a specimen of a black unctuous substance". A Professor Anderson examined these materials. He concluded that the bones were human, "subjected to the action of fire", but gave no firm opinion about the unctuous substance.

Local tradition tells of village children drawing on the stones with charcoal found at the time. Today's archaeologists inevitably regret that the cairn contents are not available for examination by modern scientific methods.

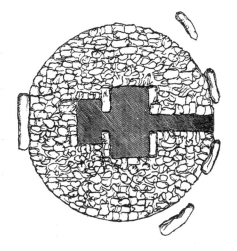

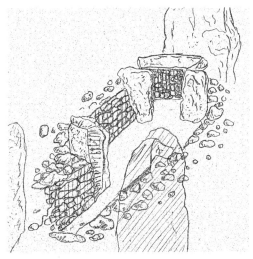

Two Surveyors and a Vicar
visitors with an artistic eye

With the discovery of the cairn at Callanish in 1857, a visit to the site became a must for all with an interest in the antiquities of Scotland. Over the following years, new records of the site were made by various visitors.

Captain F. W. L. Thomas, a prominent member of the Society of Antiquaries, undertook a surveying expedition to Callanish and nearby sites soon after the peat clearance. A fascinating series of delicate pencil drawings of individual stones are attributed to his artist-assistant, known only as 'Mr Sharbau'.

Artistically enhanced copies of Sharbau's faint originals are reproduced overleaf, while his sketch of the cairn appears on page 21. He used his own numbering system for the stones, but the accepted Somerville numbers replace them here (note that stones 36-44 are not included as they are parts of the cairn.)

Sharbau recorded stone 35 as fallen but it had been re-erected, probably at Matheson's instruction, by the time of Sir Henry James's visit. He was Director-General of the Ordnance Survey and his massive tome *Plans and Photographs of Stonehenge and Turusachan in the Island of Lewis* was published in 1867. It included the most accurate plan of Callanish then available.

Of much greater interest today, however, is the attractive 'zincograph' of the circle stones (*opposite*). Ten years after the

Copied in Chalk by 2nd Corporal Goodwin R.E.

TURUSACHAN, CALLERNISH,
OR
THE PLACE OF PILGRIMAGE ON THE BLEAK HEADLAND,
IN THE
ISLE OF LEWIS.

acidic peat had been cleared away, its bleaching effect was still clearly visible. This supports all the earlier evidence for the stones having been half-engulfed in five feet of peat. The illustration also shows the cavity of the cairn, but in a 'cosmetically tidy' state.

Rev. G. R. Mackarness, who later became Bishop of Argyll and the Isles, had visited in 1866. His careful sketch of the circle (*see page 58*) inexplicably shows the bleached sections of the stones darker, rather than lighter, than the rest.

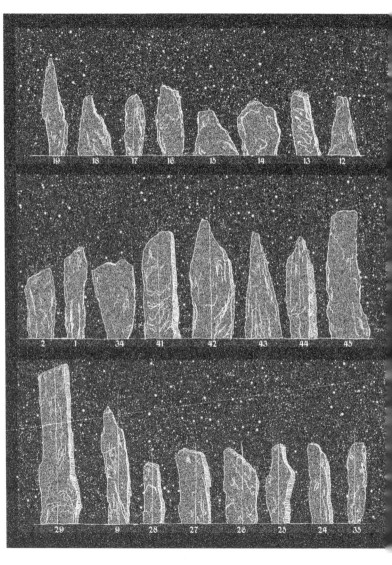

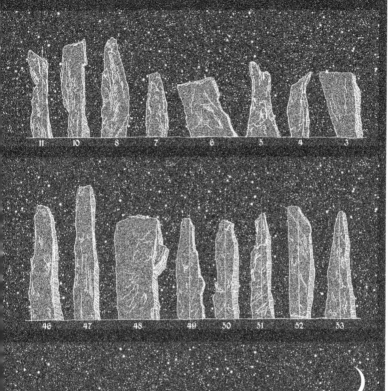

THE REDISCOVERY OF STONE 33A
buried for over one hundred years

Sharbau drew 48 stones. Today there are 49. The extra stone, part of the east row, was discovered during research by Margaret Curtis and myself.

A plan by John Lynton Palmer is dated 1857 (*opposite, top*); it was probably drawn shortly before the peat clearance. Palmer recorded the distance between each stone and the next. We checked his measurements and found them remarkably accurate. The diagram (*opposite, centre*) is based on Palmer's plan of the east row.

It appeared that he had seen a stone, additional to those known, nineteen feet beyond stone 33. Also, Callender's earlier engraving showed what could have been a fallen stone in roughly the same position (*bottom right corner of picture on page 17*).

In February 1977, we carried out a systematic survey of the relevant area with a metal probe. This proved that the stone was still beneath the soil, just outside the site fence. We named the re-discovered stone 33A.

It was uncovered during the 1980 excavation. Two years later, after the site boundary had been moved to include it, the stone was re-erected in its original socket hole, restoring the east row to its full complement of five stones (*opposite, below*).

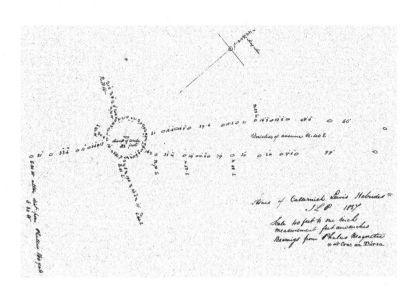

Stones of Callernish Lewis Hebrides
J.L.O. 1857
Scale 40 feet to one inch
measurement feet and inches
Bearings from Pholus Magnetic
* at Croc an Tursa

30   31   32   33   33A

THE PROTECTION OF CALLANISH
the Inspector calls

In order to support Parliamentary approval of an Ancient Monuments Protection Bill, C.P. Kains-Jackson produced *Our Ancient Monuments and the Land Around Them* (1880). This was a descriptive catalogue of important sites throughout Britain which might be scheduled under a new Act. The three-page account of Callanish includes an attractive sketch (*opposite, top*), but with many of the stones drawn out of proportion.

Once the Act was passed, in 1882, General Augustus Pitt-Rivers was appointed Inspector of Ancient Monuments. He could justifiably be called 'the father of British archaeology', having performed meticulous and accurately-recorded excavations of many sites on his own Dorset estate.

His visit to Lewis in August 1885 marks a turning-point in the story of Callanish. He was accompanied by his artist-assistant, Tomkin (*who drew the sketch opposite below*). As well as a detailed plan they made individual drawings of each stone, showing the former peat level (*example on page 14*). Stone 35, re-erected in the 1860s, was now broken, with the upper half lying alongside the erect stump (*seen in drawing on page 31*). Pitt-Rivers requested its repair, but this was delayed until the 1900s.

In addition, Pitt-Rivers negotiated the future protection of Callanish under the new Act.

The Callernish Stones
Isle of Lewis

VISITORS FROM THE CASTLE
eerie noises in the midsummer mist

One of Pitt-Rivers' roles was to persuade landowners to place 'their' monuments under government Guardianship. He had the advantage of being on equal terms with people like Lady Mary Jane Matheson of Lews Castle, by this time the owner of Lewis. In a letter to Pitt-Rivers she wrote:

> "I shall only be too glad to have the Callernish Stones …put under the Ancient Monts. Act and quite believe it is the only way to preserve them."

The path seen in John Sinclair's 1891 engraving (*opposite above*) was probably laid for the convenience of house-guests from Lews Castle. A story from this period tells of a visit made by an all-male group to see the midsummer sunrise – girls were not allowed to go, as couples sometimes became engaged at the Stones.

An old Callanish lady, from a family who were 'of the Stones', warned them before they set off that 'only those to whom it is given may see'. Though the weather was clear as the party left and returned to Stornoway, at Callanish the stones were enveloped in a thick mist, from which eerie noises emerged.

This and other stories and legends were recorded in 1966 by Otta Swire in her book *The Outer Hebrides and Their Legends* (*illustrations, opposite below and title page, both from this book*).

AMAZING LEGENDS OF THE STONES
cuckoos, wrens, witches and a magic cow

A legend common to many British circles is that the megaliths are people who were turned to stone for some transgression. At Callanish, the story is that St Kieran literally petrified pagan giants who were meeting to oppose Christianity.

Several tales involve birds: the first cuckoo of Spring traditionally gave its first call from the stones. A cuckoo's call also heralded the mysterious 'Shining One' who is said to have walked up the avenue at midsummer sunrise. Wrens always flew alongside the chief priest, who wore a cloak of coloured feathers. He and his fellow priests were supposed to have originally brought the stones to Lewis in many ships.

In another story a Gaelic-speaking cow came to the stones during a famine and gave milk to all, but a witch used a bottomless bucket to milk her dry. The cow was not seen again.

Another legend tells of a local girl who asked a witch for a magical belt to harm her rival in love. Thinking better of this evil act she disposed of the belt by wrapping it around one of the stones. At once the stone was enveloped in flames and broke in two, amid noises of howling and flapping wings.

At Beltane (May 1st) tradition was that all fires were to be extinguished on the island. An old priest then produced fire from a nearby tree and redistributed it from within the circle.

TURUSACHAN CALLERNISH

AS SEEN UNDER THE INFLUENCE OF SPIRITS

*This remarkable adaptation of James's engraving (see page 23) is to be found
in an album in the Library of St Andrew's University. The unknown artist
has adapted the stones of the circle into anthropomorphic figures, while stone
30, being shorter, becomes a seat for a fiddler. The Gaelic word for the
standing stones, Tursachan, is often taken to mean 'place of sadness'.*

BEYOND THE FRINGE
the Sleeping Beauty as the White Goddess

A range of hills in south-east Lewis takes on the appearance of a supine woman only when seen from the Callanish area (*see below*). She is called the Sleeping Beauty and, less flatteringly, Cailleach na Mointeach, the old woman of the moors.

The idea that this 'figure' had a connection with the Callanish sites arose out of astronomical research by Margaret Curtis and myself. At significant times in the lunar cycle, the moon rises from this part of the southern horizon (*see pages 44-45*).

For a certain type of visitor, stone circles emanate an indefinable mystical aura, perhaps captured in Gail Kelly's artistic interpretation of Ceann Hulavig (*opposite, below*).

Esoteric researchers have enthusiastically adopted the Sleeping Beauty as a representation of the 'White Goddess' or the 'universal Earth Mother'. Some believe that ceremonies relating to birth, fertility and death took place in the Callanish circle - rousing the White Goddess and revitalising the island and its people.

SOME THEORIES ABOUT CALLANISH
a 'rude astronomical observatory'?

Callanish has been explained in many ways. Different writers said that it was the 'supreme court of the Hebridean monarch', a resting place of the illustrious dead, an ancient gothic court, or a temple to Thor or Apollo. To many it was 'the great Druidical Cathedral of Scotland'. In 1831, Logan imagined Scottish Druids as seen opposite, but the cult probably never reached the Hebrides. In any case, stone circles were built at least a millennium before the time of the Druids.

John Toland suggested in 1726 that the 'twelve obelisks of the circle' represented the signs of the Zodiac while the 'nineteen stones on each side of the avenue' related to the 19-year lunar cycle. The stone rows related to the four principal winds.

In 1808, James Headrick called Callanish a 'rude astronomical observatory' where priests marked out the rising of the sun, moon and stars. Henry Callender claimed that the south row and the central pillar lined up with the Pole Star – but there was no star in that position in Neolithic times.

These early suggestions that there was a connection between Callanish and the heavens foreshadowed a more scientific approach to astronomy and the stones in the twentieth century. Sir Norman Lockyer, working from previous studies in 1909, claimed to have discovered two star alignments, but few researchers accept alignments with stars today.

ASTRONOMY AT THE STONES
Admiral Somerville and Professor Thom

Admiral Boyle Somerville surveyed Callanish and in 1912 published the most accurate plan up to that date (*opposite*). His numbering of the stones remains in use today (*pages 3, 24-25*). Of the astronomical alignments which he claimed, the most significant was the line from stone 9 to stone 34, which 'points' to the moonrise at its furthest north. This was the first suggestion that prehistoric man might have followed the complex movements of the moon.

Alexander Thom, a Professor of Engineering at Oxford, spent many years surveying standing stone sites throughout Britain. The original observation which stimulated his interest was made on a summer evening in 1923, when he had anchored his yacht near Callanish. Decades later, he explained:

> '... after dinner, we went ashore to explore ... I saw by looking at the Pole Star that there was a north/south line in the complex ... I wondered whether the alignment ... had been deliberately built that way ...'

Thom's eventual conclusions, which created a furore in archaeology, were that the builders of stone circles used the same system of measurement and geometry throughout Britain and that they possessed a detailed knowledge of astronomy.

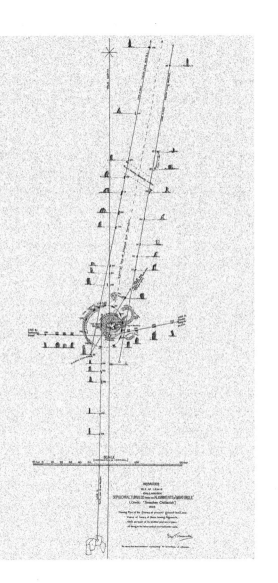

HEBRIDES
ISLE OF LEWIS
CALLANISH
SEPULCHRAL TUMULUS WITH ITS ALIGNMENTS AND GREAT CIRCLE
(Gaelic: "Tursachan Chalanish.")
1865

SCALE
(HORIZONTAL & VERTICAL)

Megalithic Science
measurement, geometry and astronomy

Thom concluded that stone rings were often constructed in geometrical shapes. He classified the central circle at Callanish as a Type A Flattened Circle. Callanish II and Callanish X also fit the same geometry, while sites II and IV are both ellipses. Callanish VIII is an unique site, with a sheer cliff-edge forming the diameter of a 'stone semi-circle'!

Thom theorised that the circle builders used a unit equal to 2.72 feet, naming it the Megalithic Yard. According to Ron Curtis's survey, Callanish IV has a long axis of 15 MY, a short axis of 12 MY and a perimeter of just over $42\frac{1}{2}$ MY.

Although Thom's specific ideas on astronomy at Callanish have been largely superseded, his books stimulated the new discipline of archaeo-astronomy. Stone alignments are checked to see if the builders lined them up with prominent horizon features where the sun or moon rises or sets at the time of significant astronomical events.

Details of the six surveys shown opposite:

Site I - after Thom's version of Somerville's survey. Geometry from Curtis.

Sites II, III and IV - Compound images, after Curtis and Thom.

Site VIII - Ponting, after Glasgow University Geography Dept. survey.

Site X - Survey and geometry after Curtis.

Arrows indicate Curtis' suggested inter-site alignments.

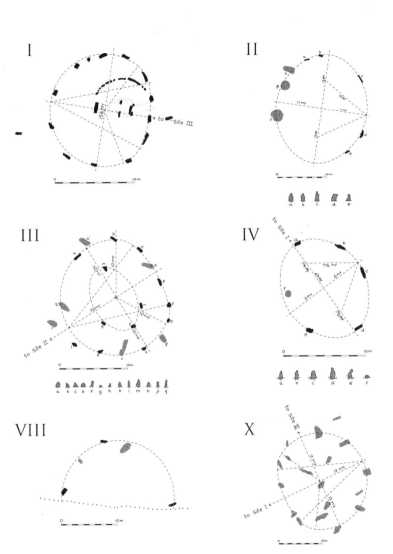

41

A LITTLE BASIC ASTRONOMY
the movements of the Sun and Moon

The sun rises in the east and sets in the west – but this is only strictly true at the equinoxes in March and September.

In summer the sun's rising and setting positions on the horizon are well to the north of due east and west; in winter they are to the south. At the northerly latitude of Callanish, these seasonal swings are more pronounced than in southern England (*see illustration opposite*).

The moon's rising and setting positions on the horizon undergo a similar variation over each lunar month, but the extent of the swing around the horizon varies over a cycle lasting 18.6 years. The largest swings occur at the 'major standstills', as in 1987, 2006 and 2025. Midway in the 18.6-year cycle (the 'minor standstill'), the moon's swings are less pronounced than those of the sun.

At the 'northern extreme of major standstill' the moon rises and sets further north than the sun ever reaches, setting behind the horizon only briefly (*the longest arc, opposite*). At the 'southern extreme of major standstill' the moon barely rises (*shortest arc, opposite*).

At the latitude of Callanish, this event is especially spectacular, with the moon skimming the southern horizon, as seen in the illustration on the next double page.

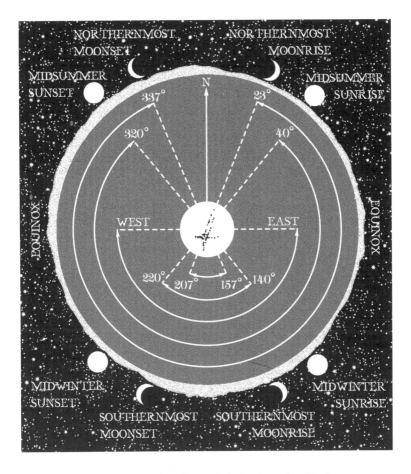

*Figures are azimuths - degrees clockwise from True North -
and assume a horizon with zero altitude.*

PREHISTORIC TEMPLES
why were stone circles built?

Various roles have been suggested for sites like Callanish. They include observatories, temples (perhaps with a funerary purpose), calendrical markers and tribal 'status symbols'. Stone circles could well have served all of these purposes and more.

'Primitive' cultures tend to combine all aspects of their lives, including religion, art, medicine, astronomy and farming, in a single ritual framework. Construction of a circle must have been a communal effort which aided social cohesion. When complete, it was probably a social and religious centre with purposes not dissimilar to those of a medieval parish church.

Whatever deity was worshipped (Sun, Moon or 'Earth Mother'), ceremonies in the circle probably included harvest celebrations, initiation, fertility and funeral rites, even trading.

Officiating 'priests' may have had detailed knowledge of the

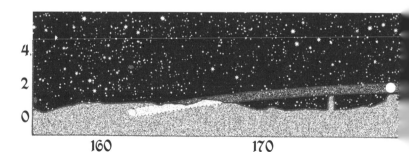

movements of sun and moon, handed down as oral tradition and preserved in megalithic structures. Thus the best times for impressive ceremonies would have been known.

Two classical Greek writers wrote about the northern region of 'Hyperborea'. Eratosthenes said the Hyperboreans' temple was 'winged', while in 55 BC Diodorus wrote:

> '...there is also on the island ... a notable temple which is ... spherical in shape ... the moon, as viewed from this island, appears but a little distance from the earth ... the god visits the island every nineteen years...'

The facts fit Callanish well. For spherical, read circular, while the east and west rows could be the 'wings'; 19 years is close enough to 18.6; for the god, read the moon, which does remain 'a little distance from the earth' at its southern extreme.

In June 1987, observers standing in the avenue witnessed this extreme lunar event as the full moon rose out of the Sleeping Beauty, skimmed the horizon, and set briefly, before re-appearing 'among' the stones of the circle (*shown below*).

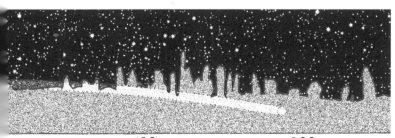

190   200

CNOC CEANN A' GHARRAIDH
Callanish II

At the end of a cul-de-sac road, about half a mile to the south-west of Callanish, stands another fascinating circle of stones, often referred to as 'Callanish II'. Its Gaelic name, pronounced approximately 'croc kyain a gaa-ree', means the hillock at the end of the wall. There are five erect stones, one standing almost ten feet high, plus four or more fallen slabs.

As the 'minor site' nearest the 'main site', this circle was recorded by several antiquarian visitors. After the success of the peat clearance at the main Callanish site, Sir James Matheson had the peat cleared from sites II, III and IV in the following year. (*See location map, page 55*).

John Stuart's bird's eye view drawing (*shown opposite*) clearly shows a cairn and other internal features which were revealed in 1858, shortly before his visit.

Stuart's paper was called *Notes of Incised Marks on one of a Circle of Standing Stones*. He believed, rather gullibly, that a particular stone was marked with deliberate characters, perhaps even Ogham script! Undoubtedly, these were naturally occurring cracks. (It is the rounded stone, lying a little below the centre of the circle.) The stone is said to have been moved to Sir James' estate in Stornoway for protection. If so, it was later partially broken up as building material.

1. Stone with supposed Inscription on its side
2. Cairn or heap of small stones
3, 4, 5, 6, Small pits in which charcoal was found
7, 8, Flat stones

BIRDS EYE SKETCH OF STANDING STONES

About a mile from the large stone Circle near Callernish Island of Lewis.

Proceedings of the Society of Antiquaries of Scotland

CALLANISH III & IV
Cnoc Fillibhir Bheag & Cean Hulavig

The Gaelic name of Callanish III, pronounced 'croc filiver vegg', means little Fillivir hillock. Eight stones stand erect, with another four standing within the ring, as shown in Admiral Somerville's survey (*opposite, above*). There are also several fallen stones.

Being clearly visible from the road when approaching Callanish from Stornoway, it is certainly the most visited of the so-called minor sites. In modern times, the circle seems to attract the more mystically-inclined visitor, who may regret the modern intrusion of interpretive notices and a hard surrounding path at Callanish itself. On a stormy winter day in 1984, the Glaswegian rock band, Ultravox, made a pop video here.

About $1\frac{1}{4}$ miles to the south lies Ceann Hulavig ('kyain hoo-la-vig', head of Hula bay, Callanish IV). This is a less accessible site, but a fascinating one, with five tall stones, all encrusted with hoary lichen, standing on an ellipse (*see Gail Kelly's engraving on page 35*).

When peat was removed here in the late 1850s only the area within the stones was cleared, with the result that they stand around a poorly-drained hollow, as shown in Tomkin's sketch (*opposite, below*).

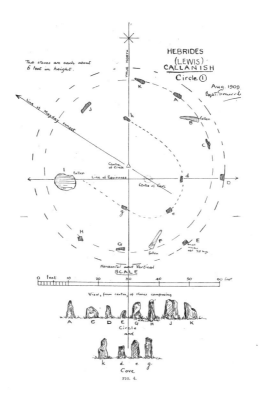

The stones are each about 6 feet in height.

HEBRIDES (LEWIS) CALLANISH
Circle ①

Aug. 1909

Line of May-day sunset

Line of Equinoxes

Centre of Circle

Centre of Cave

K A B fallen C k J l fallen d D g e H G F fallen E

Horizontal and Vertical SCALE

0 feet 10 20 30 40 50 60 feet

View, from centre, of stones composing
A C D E G H J K
Circle and
k d e g
Cove

FIG. 4.

INDEPENDENT OR INTER-RELATED ?
reasons for numerous sites in one area

Why are so many standing stone sites concentrated around Callanish, and what was the connection between them? There are various suggestions.

- The sites are of different periods, each being constructed as an improvement upon the previous one.

- Each site was the temple of a branch of the ancient religion, in the same way that each Christian sect has its own churches.

- Each circle was the focus of a small community. This has been shown to be likely in, for example, the Lands End area. If each small ring was, in episcopalian terms, a 'parish church', then Callanish itself must have been the 'cathedral'.

- All the sites were in use at the same time and formed an interdependent complex, perhaps with sight-lines between them having astronomical significance. This idea is implicit in the concept of the 'Callanish diamond' (*opposite*), with all the sites being in an area where two ranges of hills relate to the rise and set of the moon at its most extreme southerly position.

Callanish still keeps many of its secrets, despite the best efforts of eighteenth and nineteenth-century antiquarians and twentieth-century archaeologists and astronomers. The techniques of the future may reveal some of the site's mysteries, but will not destroy the fascination of 'the Stonehenge of the Hebrides'.

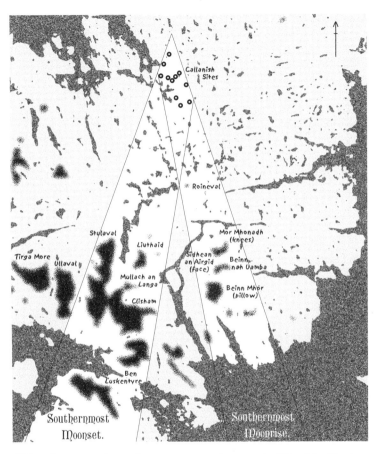

When the moon at its southernmost extreme rises over the hills of the Sleeping
Beauty and sets into the Harris hills, the viewing lines for moonrise and
moonset form a 'diamond', within which all the Callanish sites lie. Could
this be the reason why so many sites are found in this area?

SITES ON LEWIS AND HARRIS

This list, continuing over the next five pages, records brief details of standing stone sites that are likely to date from the Neolithic and Bronze Age periods. A few of the more important chambered cairns are listed, but these are so numerous, especially on North Uist, and often so ruinous, that most are omitted. The inclusion of a site does not imply that access is permitted – always check locally if in doubt. Avoid disturbing sheep and cattle and respect the islanders' wish to observe the Sabbath.

LEWIS

Clach Stein comprises two stones at Knockaird, Ness. [NB 535642]

Clach Stei Lin is a 5 ft tall megalith near Lower Shader. Other slabs nearby may have been part of a larger setting. [NB 397 545]

Steinacleit is a complex site above Shader township with ten erect stones and others fallen. It may represent a ruined burial cairn, adapted to other uses in later generations. [NB 396 541]

Clach an Trushal. The impressive 19 ft 'Thrushel Stone' at Ballantrushal is probably the tallest single megalith in Scotland. [NB 376 537]

Clach an Trushal

Clach an Cnoc Laorain (Loch Roinavat Stone Circle), near Shawbost, was first recorded in 1983 by Margaret Curtis. There are two erect slabs and a number of less obvious features. [NB 233 463]

Clach an Tursa ('stones of sadness') is within the croftland of Upper Carloway. It was probably once an alignment, but only one megalith still stands, almost 7 feet tall. Two other stones lie, broken, nearby. [NB 204 430]

Achmore Stone Circle is a true circle of about 45 yards diamter, one of the largest in Scotland. There are about 20 stones of which two are erect. The site was first recorded by Margaret Curtis and myself in 1981, after we had removed the overlying peat from some of the stones. [NB 317 292]

Druim Dubh Stone Circle. Sixteen prone slabs, some almost buried, lie in an ellipse across the road from the Half Way Garage. First recorded by Margaret Curtis in 1992. [NB 357 274]

Priest's Glen is a ruinous stone circle near New Valley. [NB 411 351]

Clach Stein, near Bayble, is a prone slab which once stood about ten feet high. [NB 517 317]

Loch Seaforth (Fangs, Sideval) is marked as 'Stone Circle, remains of' on the OS map. It was much modified in later centuries. [NB 278 167]

… plus all the Callanish area sites (in the boxed area) which are shown on pages 54-55.

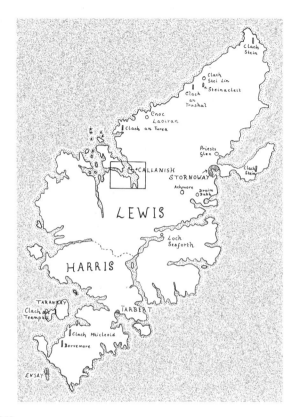

HARRIS

Clach an Teampuill is a 5 ft tall stone on the island of Taransay (famous from BBC TV's Castaway). It bears an inscribed cross, perhaps Christianising a pagan monument. [NB 013 008]

Clach Mhic Leoid is a prominent 10 ft stone, overlooking the shore at Nisabost. [NG 041 972]

Borvemore Standing Stone (Scarista) stands $6\frac{1}{2}$ feet high on the machair near Borvemore village and may be the remains of a circle. [NG 021 939]

A 5 ft tall standing stone on the uninhabited island of **Ensay**, Sound of Harris. [NF 981 868]

SITES AROUND CALLANISH

1. **The Standing Stones of Callanish (Callanish I,** *Tursachan, Calanais, 'the Stonehenge of the Hebrides')* [NB 213 330]. *Nearby Visitor Centre - exhibition, shop, cafe and toilets.*

2. **Cnoc Ceann a' Gharraidh (Callanish II,** *' Loch Roag')* [NB 222 326] – *see pages 46-47.*

3. **Cnoc Fillibhir Bheag (Callanish III)** [NB 225 327] – *see pages 48-49.*

4. **Ceann Hulavig (Callanish IV,** *'Garynahine')* [NB 230 304] – *see page 48-49.*

5. **Airigh nam Bidearan** *('sheiling of the pinnacles',* **Callanish V)** *lies in peaty moorland, SW of Garynahine. Three stones stand in line, each less than 3 feet high, more stones lying or buried in the peat. The alignment indicates moonrise at its extreme southern position.* [NB 234 299]

6. **Cul a' Chleit (Callanish VI)** – *two standing stones, 3 ft and $5\frac{1}{2}$ ft tall, on a hillock beyond site V.* [NB 247 303]

7. **Cnoc Dubh** - *Thom's* **Callanish VII** *but probably not prehistoric* [NB 232 302] .

8. **Cleitir (Callanish VIII,** *Barraglom, Bernera Bridge)* *stands on the island of Great Bernera, overlooking the bridge. The tallest of the three erect stones is 9 ft high; others are fallen or buried. This is an unusual (perhaps unique) 'stone semi-circle', facing south on a cliff-edge.* [NB 164 342]

8a. **Aird a' Chaolais (Callanish VIIIA)** *is a single stone, near the opposite shore, overthrown when a road was widened.* [NB 165 340]

9. **Druim nan Bidearan (Callanish IX)** - *two prone slabs by a modern cairn* [NB233 297]

10. **Na Dromannan (Callanish X,** *'Druim nan Eum')* *is situated on a moorland ridge east of Callanish village. Nineteen or more large fallen slabs seem to have once formed a circle with both outlying stones and internal features. The nearby rocky cliff is reputed to be the quarry from which the stones at the main Callanish site were obtained.* [NB 230 336]

11. **Airigh na Beinne Bige (Callanish XI)** *a single erect stone, almost 5 ft high, others fallen or buried by peat. It stands on a ridge with a superb view over the whole Callanish area.* [NB 222 356]

12. *At the entrance to* **Stonefield** *in Breasclete stands a single $3\frac{1}{2}$ ft stone* **(Callanish XII)** *which was left in place and set in a cobbled plinth when the houses were built in the 1960s.* [NB 215 350]

13. **Sgeir nan Each (Callanish XIII)** - *a thin prone slab on the sea-shore* [NB 215 341].

14. **Cnoc Sgeir na h'Uidhe (Callanish XIV)** *is a small erect stone, situated such that the sun rises directly above it at the equinoxes, as viewed from Callanish I.* [NB 228 329]

15. **Airigh Mhaoldonuich (Callanish XV)** *may once have stood over 11 feet high. Today it lies*

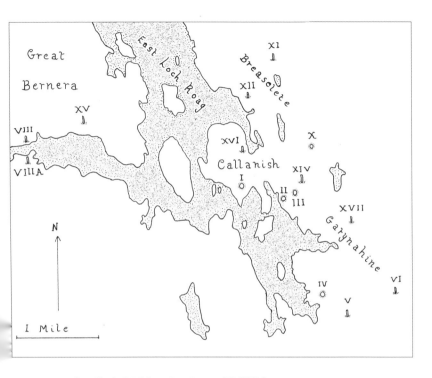

prone in the croftland of Kirkibost, Great Bernera. [NB 177 346]

16. **Cliacabhaigh (Callanish XVI)**, a single stone about 3 feet high. It is almost due north of the central stone at Callanish I and in line with the central stone and south row. [NB 213 338]

17. **Druim na h'Aon Chloich** (the 'ridge of the one stone', **Callanish XVII**), a single broken prone slab on a hillside at Garynahine. Viewed from this spot, site IV lines up with the 'notch' in the Harris hills and the re-gleam of the moon at its southern extreme. [NB 237 320]

18. **Loch Crogach (Callanish XVIII)** - a small erect stone [NB 244 292]

19. **Buaile Chruaidh (Callanish XIX)** - the broken base of a single stone [NB 218 331]

N.B. There is no confirmation that some of the sites given Callanish numbers are prehistoric. Sites VII, IX, XIII, XVIII and XIX are omitted from the map for this reason.

SITES IN THE UISTS AND BARRA

NORTH UIST

Cladh Maolrithe, *standing stone at Borve on Berneray, between Harris and North Uist (not on map below). [NF 912 807]*

1. **Crois Mhic Jamain**, *standing stones at Port nan Long. [NF 894 782]*

2. **Clach an t-Sagairt** *near Clachan Sands, with an inscribed cross. [NF 878 760]*

3. **Maari** *Standing Stone [NF 864 729]*

4. **Na Fir Bhreige** *('the false men') are on the slope of Blashaval three miles west of Lochmaddy. The stones, of which only about 3 feet protrudes above the peat, are said to have been three men who deserted their wives on Skye and were punished by being turned to stone by a witch. [NF 887 717]*

5. **Leac nan Cailleachan Dubha**, *two large standing stones on the tidal island of Vallay. [NF 791 765]*

Leac nan Cailleachan Dubha

6. **South Clettreval**, *two st. stones; a chambered cairn adapted as an Iron Age house. [NF 751 712]*

7. **Bheinn a' Charra**, *a huge 11 ft slab, on the hillside near Committee Road. [NF 786 691]*

8. **Toroghas**, *two st. stones on a hillside 500 yds N of Loch Mhic Gille-Bhride. [NF 770 703]*

N. UIST

9. Clach Mhor a' Che, *a single 8 ft stone, close to the shore near Westford Inn. [NF 770 662]*

10. Leacach an Tigh Cloiche, *SW shoulder of Unival, remains of a chambered cairn with nine stones still erect. [NF 800 668]*

11. Barpa Langass *(Langass Barp) is the best-preserved chambered cairn in the islands. [NF 838 657]*

Langass Barp

12. Pobull Fhinn *('Fingal's People'), other side of Beinn Langass from the barp, a reasonably well-preserved 'stone oval', about 120 ft by 93 ft. Eight erect stones, c.12 prone. [NF 843 650]*

13. Sornach a' Pobull *(Loch a' Phobuill) – stone circle, 1½ miles SW of Pobull Fhinn with 13 stones standing. One is 5 ft tall, but most are small and almost hidden in the peat. [NF 829 630]*

14. *The Hill of* **Craonaval** *bears chambered cairns, a stone circle and a number of individual slabs. Ultach Fhinn ('Fingal's armful') is a huge prone slab 23 ft by 6½ ft. It may be the remains of a burial chamber. [NF 83 63]*

15. Carinish Stone Circle *is largely ruined; the A865 goes through the middle of it. [NF 832 602]*

BENBECULA

16. Gramsdale North *[NF 825 562] and* **Gramsdale South** *(Suidheachadh Sealg) [NF 825 552]. At each of these sites, ½ mile apart, only one stone remains erect, but fallen slabs suggest that both were circles.*

SOUTH UIST

17. Crois Chnoca Breaca *(Stoneybridge) – a thin leaning slab, near the shore. [NF 734 336]*

18. Bheinn a' Charra *– a 17 ft megalith. [NF 770 321]*

19. Bornish *(Sligeanach Kildonan) is said to have once stood 13 ft high but is often almost covered by the sand dunes. [NF 727 286]*

20. Pollachar Standing Stone, *on the shore near the Pollachar Inn, fell and was re-erected. [NF 745 144]*

BARRA

21. Borve Standing Stones *are situated within sand dunes. [NF 653 014]*

22. Druim a' Charra (Brevig) *is a single stone, standing high on a hillside. [NL 689 990]*

PUBLICATIONS OF INTEREST

There are many good general books about British stone circles, both popular and technical. The definitive work is the second edition of Aubrey Burl's 'The Stone Circles of the British Isles' (2000).

Publications by Gerald Ponting and Margaret Ponting/Curtis: 'The Standing Stones of Callanish', (1977, out of print); 'Achmore Stone Circle' – a full account of its discovery (1981); 'New Light on the Stones of Callanish', 56-page guide book (1984); 'The Stones Around Callanish', a field guide to the 'minor sites' (1984). Also technical papers : 'Decoding the Callanish Complex - some initial results' in 'Astronomy and Society in Britain' (Ruggles and Whittle, 1981) and 'Decoding the Callanish Complex - a progress report' in 'Archaeoastronomy in the Old World' (Heggie, 1984). Two unpublished reports, 'Callanish, the Documentary Record' (1979) and 'CDR 2 - the minor sites' (1981), are available for consultation in Stornoway Library.

Also recommended: 'Callanish - Stones, Moon and Sacred Landscape' by Ron and Margaret Curtis (1994) and 'Some Geometry Associated [with] Callanish' by G.R. Curtis in Hebridean Naturalist (1979); 'Callanish' by Patrick Ashmore in 'Studies in Scottish Antiquity' (Breeze, 1984); also the official site guide-book, 'Calanais - the Standing Stones' (Ashmore, 1995); Ashmore's excavation report on Callanish (forthcoming).

Full bibliographical details of all antiquarian material used in this book are available via the following page on the web: www.megalithic.co.uk/callanish-bibliography.